P9-DYP-709

WHAT'S INSIDE THIS BACKPACK?

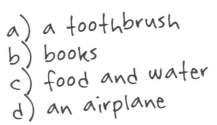

a) a toothbrush
b) books
c) food and water
d) an airplane

If you picked d, you're right. It's an airplane!

And it's not just any plane. This is the Dragon Eye. It's a small spy plane. It's only three feet (0.9 m) long, and it flies without a pilot.

It's so small a soldier can carry it in his or her backpack. Once it's in the air, it can find the enemy and send back pictures.

Keep reading to find out about more super-small spy planes.

Book design Red Herring Design/NYC

Library of Congress Cataloging-in-Publication Data
Rudy, Lisa Jo, 1960–
Micro spies : spy planes the size of a birds! / Lisa Jo Rudy.
p. cm. — 24/7 : science behind the scenes
Includes bibliographical references and index.
ISBN-13: 978-0-531-12083-5 (lib. bdg.)   978-0-531-17535-4 (pbk.)
ISBN-10: 0-531-12083-X (lib. bdg.)   0-531-17535-9 (pbk.)
1. Micro air vehicles—Juvenile literature. 2. Reconnaissance
aircraft—Juvenile literature. 3. Airplanes—Models—Juvenile
literature. I. Title.
UG1242.R4.R83 2007
623.74'69—dc22   2006021232

Published simultaneously in Canada. Printed in the United States of America.

SCHOLASTIC, FRANKLIN WATTS, and associated logos are trademarks
and/or registered trademarks of Scholastic Inc.
1 2 3 4 5 6 7 8 9 10 R 17 16 15 14 13 12 11 10 09 08

MICRO SPIES

Spy Planes the Size of Birds!

Lisa Jo Rudy

WARNING: Unmanned Aerial Vehicles (UAVs) are often used during war. They're also used to fight crime. So if you don't want to read about war or crime, this book is not for you!

Franklin Watts
An Imprint of Scholastic Inc.
New York • Toronto • London • Auckland • Sydney
Mexico City • New Delhi • Hong Kong
Danbury, Connecticut

CONTENTS

In these true stories, you'll see the world's highest-flying spies in action.

The Predator and other high-tech spy planes take off.

17

Case #1:
Strike from the Sky!

From the Predator to the Global Hawk to the Dragon Eye, UAVs are keeping the military armed—and pilots out of harm.

Case #2:
Sky High

UAVs can soar in domestic skies, too. They can fight forest fires, find lost kids, and even catch crooks.

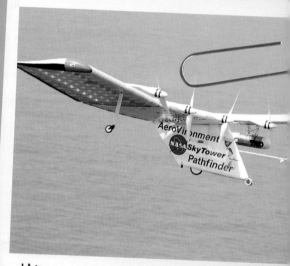

Will unmanned aerial vehicles change civilian life?

Case #3:
Robo-Flies

Get out your magnifying glass. These tiny spies are the biggest thing in UAVs.

35

Engineers compete to build the smallest spy planes.

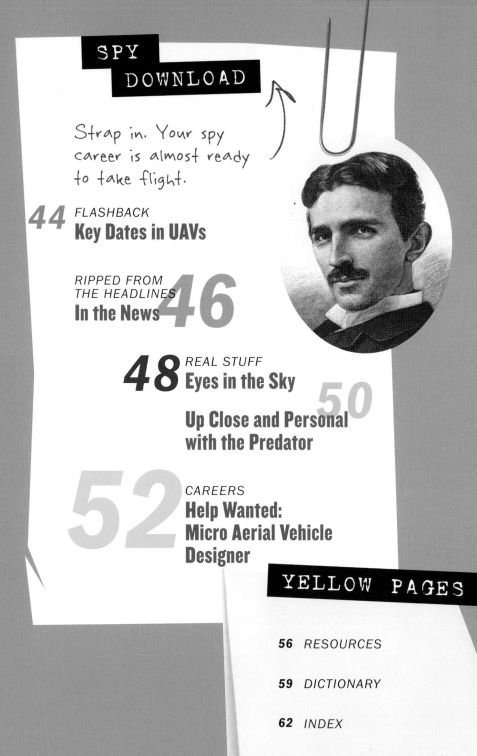

SPY DOWNLOAD

Strap in. Your spy career is almost ready to take flight.

YELLOW PAGES

They're as big as jet planes—or as small as birds. They can cover the skies—or fit into your pocket. They can go to war—or save you from disaster.

SPY 411

They're Unmanned Aerial Vehicles (UAVs). They're high-tech military tools. They're a criminal's worst nightmare. And they're the latest in disaster relief.

IN THIS SECTION:

- ▶ learn how UAV experts really talk;
- ▶ meet the world's greatest UAVs;
- ▶ find out who's on the same team as the drones.

UAV Talk

Experts who work with UAVs have their own way of talking. Find out what their vocabulary means.

UAV
(YOO-aye-vee) an aircraft with no pilot onboard. A UAV can fly by remote control, or it can follow a pre-programmed flight plan. UAV is short for *unmanned aerial vehicle.*

This mission is too dangerous for human pilots. We need to send a **UAV** to get the **intelligence** we need.

intelligence
(in-TEL-uh-jens) information about an enemy or a possible enemy

These UAVs just keep getting smaller. Have you seen that new **MAV**? It will be excellent for **reconnaissance.**

MAV
(EM-aye-vee) a UAV that is super-small and controlled by radio. MAV is short for *micro aerial vehicle.*

"Micro" means "small." "Aerial" means "in the air."

reconnaissance
(ree-KOHN-uh-sins) the collection of intelligence, usually by inspection or secret observation

The micro UAV is amazing. But as an engineer, I dream of building an ornithopter.

engineer
(en-jihn-EER) a person who uses scientific knowledge to solve problems

ornithopter
(ORN-ih-thop-tur) an airplane that flies the way birds fly. Ornithopters have wings that flap.

"Orni" has to do with birds.

I know what you mean. We can build smaller and smaller UAVs. But we still don't fully understand the aeronautics of birds.

aeronautics
(ayr-oh-NAW-tiks) the study of flight and aircraft

"Nautic" has to do with sailing and ships.

Say What?

Here's some more lingo related to MAVs.

backpackable
(BAK-pak-uh-buhl) small and light enough to carry in a backpack
*"The **backpackable** MAV could be carried by soldiers into enemy territory."*

bungee
(BUHN-jee) a stretchy cord sometimes used to launch MAVs
*"The soldiers pulled the Dragon Eye UAV from his backpack and launched it into the air with a **bungee** cord."*

drone
(drone) a plane that is controlled by a ground pilot with a joystick
*"The **drone** was sent to gather intelligence."*

infrared
(IN-frah-rehd) describing a camera that can work in the dark
*"The spies used the **infrared** camera to film the enemy camp at night."*

Meet the UAVs

Some are smaller than a candy bar. Others are bigger than a bus. Take a look at the latest in high-tech spy planes.

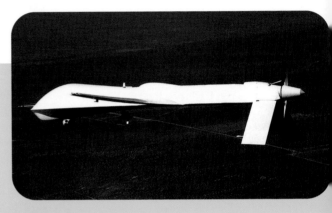

PREDATOR

What Is It? One of the most famous—and most effective—UAVs. First designed as a spy plane, the Predator now carries two laser-guided Hellfire **missiles** for attacks.

How Does It Work? The Predator is controlled by pilots on the ground, sometimes thousands of miles away. They operate it with a **joystick** and watch its movement on video screens.

Pros: It can spy and attack. And it can stay in the air for more than 24 hours.

Cons: The Predator crashes—a lot. It has trouble in bad weather, particularly icy conditions. And it takes about 55 people on the ground to control one plane.

STATS
Length: 27 feet (8.3 m)
Height: 6.9 feet (2.1 m)
Weight: 1,130 pounds (513 kg)
Wingspan: 48.7 feet (14.8 m)
Speed: Up to 135 mph (217.3 kph)
Ceiling: It can fly as high as 25,000 feet (7,620 m).
Endurance: It can stay in the air for more than 24 hours.
Cost: $3 million per plane

GLOBAL HAWK

What Is It? The most sophisticated pure spy plane in the world. The Hawk flies higher than the Predator. That lowers its chance of being shot down. And it takes better pictures. But it's only for spying. There are no missiles onboard.

How Does It Work? Unlike the Predator, the Global Hawk is completely **autonomous**. That means it flies itself. It follows a pre-programmed flight plan without a ground pilot controlling.

STATS
Length: 44 feet (13.4 m)
Height: 15 feet (4.6 m)
Weight: 8,490 pounds (3,851 kg)
Wingspan: 116 feet (35.4 m)
Speed: 400 mph (643.7 kph)
Ceiling: It can fly as high as 65,000 feet (19,812 m).
Endurance: It can stay in the air for as long as 35 hours.
Cost: $40 million per plane

Pros: It flies higher, faster, and for longer periods than the Predator. It can handle rough weather, and its camera can see through cloud cover and sandstorms.

Cons: At $40 million, the Hawk is even more costly than the Predator. And it crashes even more than the Predator!

U.S. AIR FORCE

DRAGON EYE

What Is It? The world's most reliable MAV. It's fully autonomous. It's good for scouting urban areas and taking pictures without getting caught.

How Does It Work? The Dragon Eye folds into a backpack. It can be put together by a two-person team in about 10 minutes. It's launched by hand or with a bungee cord.

Pros: It is small and nearly silent. It's perfect for spying on enemies in close quarters. It can be carried by troops and launched within minutes.

Cons: Like other UAVs, it crashes too often. It's too big to hide in trees or fly into a room unnoticed. And it's only powerful enough to carry a small battery, which runs out quickly.

STATS
Length: 3 feet (0.9 m)
Weight: 5 pounds (2.3 kg)
Wingspan: 45 inches (114.3 cm)
Speed: 40 mph (64.4 kph)
Ceiling: It flies 300–500 feet (91.4–152.4 m).
Endurance: Battery operated, its charge lasts about an hour.
Cost: $60,000–70,000

BLACK WIDOW

What Is It? It may be the future of UAVs. This micro spy plane is the size of a CD. It's small and sneaky.

How Does it Work? It is powered by an electric motor and has a small **propeller** in its nose. It's controlled by a radio operator, just like a toy plane.

Pros: It's the smallest, quietest functioning micro UAV ever. It takes videos from a camera the size of a penny.

Cons: It's still in the testing stages. Its flight time is very limited. Bad weather knocks it off course.

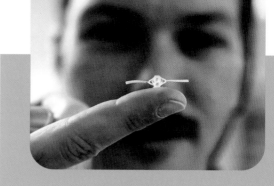

STATS

Size: Smaller than 6 inches (15.2 cm)

Weight: Less than an ounce (28 g); about the weight of a hummingbird

Speed: The fastest ornithopter has been clocked at about 50 mph (80.5 kph).

Endurance: So far, the best ornithopters can only stay aloft for about 3 to 15 minutes.

ORNITHOPTER

What Is It? A tiny plane that flies the way birds do.

How Does It Work? Ornithopters flap their wings, just like birds. This allows them to perch in trees and hover overhead. They're tossed into the air and controlled by radio.

Pros: These micro planes are a spy's dream. It takes only seconds to launch them. They can stay hidden near an enemy for days. They take pictures with a video camera in their nose. They are ultra-portable. Some fold into a matchbox-sized container.

Cons: They don't work—at least not on a big scale yet. Scientists are still trying to make an ornithopter that can stay in the air for more than just a few minutes.

STATS

Size: 6 inches (15.2 cm) wide.

Weight: 3 ounces (85 g)

Ceiling: About 600 feet (182.9 m)

Speed: 20–30 mph (32.2–48.3 kph)

Endurance: About 30 minutes

Cost: $170,000

The Spy Team

It takes more than one person to get a spy plane in the air.

RESEARCHERS
They're usually engineers. They figure out how to make UAVs that do what the military wants. They sometimes work with teams that include designers, aeronautical engineers, technicians, and computer experts.

PILOTS
They're often thousands of miles away. They operate some UAVs with a joystick and video screens. Others program autonomous UAVs to follow a flight plan.

UAVS
They're planes without pilots. But they still need plenty of people to get them off the ground. It takes as many as 82 people, including pilots, to handle some UAVs!

FABRICATORS
The people who actually build the UAVs. Their jobs include electronics, machining, mechanics, and product testing.

MILITARY SPECIALISTS
UAV experts in the armed forces. They're trained to maintain, launch, and guide UAVs. They also analyze reports from UAVs.

CONTRACTORS
Large or small companies that turn basic UAV designs into military tools. The people involved may be computer designers, engineers, aeronautical experts, or military experts.

14

TRUE-LIFE CASE FILES!

24 hours a day, 7 days a week, 365 days a year, someone out there is working on a UAV!

IN THIS SECTION:

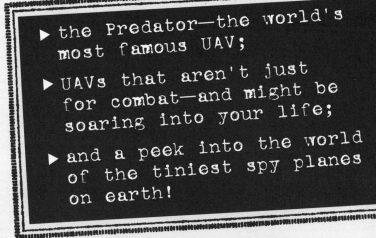

- ▶ the Predator—the world's most famous UAV;
- ▶ UAVs that aren't just for combat—and might be soaring into your life;
- ▶ and a peek into the world of the tiniest spy planes on earth!

UAVs by the Numbers

These UAVs have a special place in the record books.

Fastest UAV Ever
The D-21: Mach 4

Highest Flying UAV
Helios (*right*): 96,500 feet (29,413 m); ground launched

NASA 731, Orville 103,000 feet (31,394 m); balloon launched

Biggest UAV
Helios: 246-foot (75-m) wingspan

Heaviest UAV
Boeing 720 (*above*): 202,000 pounds (91,626 kg). This plane was made into a drone for use during crash-landing tests.

Smallest UAV
Black Widow (*left*): 6-inch (15.2-cm) wingspan; around 3 ounces (85 g)

Longest flight of a UAV
Condor: 51 hours

November 2002
the deserts of Yemen
and Nevada

Strike from the Sky!

From the Predator to the Global Hawk to the Dragon Eye, UAVs are keeping the military armed— and pilots out of harm.

The Predator

A UAV goes after terrorists in the dark of night.

It's November 2002. Under the cover of darkness, **terrorists** hide in the deserts of Yemen in the Middle East. But this time, the black night isn't enough to keep them safe.

Far over their heads, an invisible, silent killer is tracking their moves. And as the terrorists climb into a car, the attack begins.

The Predator strikes.

The Predator is a sneaky, flying fighter plane. It can track the cleverest criminals. And its Hellfire missiles are deadly accurate.

NORTH AMERICA

NEVADA UNITED STATES

In November 2002, the Predator was sent to find terrorists in the deserts of Yemen. Meanwhile, its pilot was safely on the ground in Nevada.

N
W · E
S

SOUTH AMERICA

But the Predator isn't like the jets you've seen in action movies. That's because inside the Predator's **cockpit**, no one is flying the plane.

The Predator is an unmanned aerial vehicle—or UAV. That means there's no pilot onboard.

This plane is a **remote-controlled** weapon in the sky. It has powerful cameras that can spy on enemies. It can tell the military where a terrorist is hiding.

And it can attack. Armed with Hellfire missiles, the Predator can fly into dangerous

An MQ-1 Predator armed with AGM-114 Hellfire missiles on a test flight at Nellis Air Force Base in Nevada. This plane's primary mission is conducting reconnaissance.

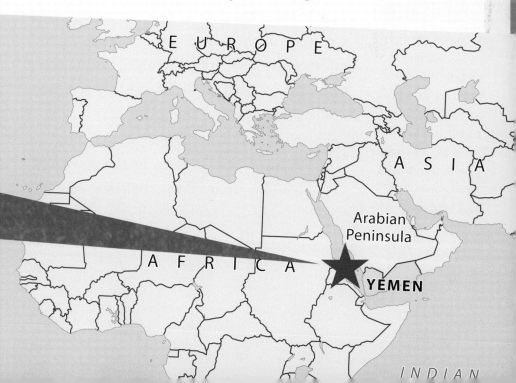

EUROPE

ASIA

Arabian Peninsula

AFRICA

YEMEN

INDIAN

These shots are from a video taken by a pilotless Predator in 2001. The images show Iraqi military firing on British or U.S. planes. These pictures were used to help build a case against Iraqi leader Saddam Hussein.

places where human pilots can't go. It can track and engage an enemy—all without putting a single soldier at risk.

That's how the Predator ended up in the air over the Yemen desert. Tracking Al Qaeda terrorists, the Predator soared over the Middle Eastern nation. But it was controlled by an Air Force pilot about 8,000 miles (12,875 km) away in Nevada. The pilot guided the plane with a joystick and watched its every motion on a video screen.

On the screen, the pilot saw his target. A group of men climbed into a car. The men were considered among the most dangerous terrorists in the world. One of them helped mastermind the 2000 bombing of a Navy destroyer called the USS *Cole*. Seventeen sailors were killed in that blast.

Using a joystick, the Predator pilot in Nevada aimed his missiles at the terrorists' car. Then he fired. Two Hellfires streaked through the air faster than the speed of sound. They hit their target with 17 pounds (7.7 kg) of high explosives.

The Predator in Action

The Predator is a technological wonder. But it's far from perfect.

The 27-foot (8.2-m) Predator is the military's first modern UAV. With its 50-foot (15.2 m) wingspan, the Predator can fly on little fuel. It can go as high as 25,000 feet (7,620 m) for as long as 24 hours. At that height, it's almost impossible for an enemy to spot it. But the Predator can see them. Its camera can take pictures from five miles (8 km) away—day or night.

Originally designed as a spy plane, the Predator can now drop bombs. Since 1995, the Predator has flown combat **missions** in Yemen, Afghanistan, and Iraq—all without risking U.S. soldiers.

It takes some highly trained teams on the ground and behind the scenes to make this happen.

During the Iraq War (beginning in 2003), for example, Predators were launched by soldiers on the ground.

Then, UAV pilots in the U.S. took over. Some of these pilots were based at Nellis Air Force Base in Nevada. There, they sat in small rooms, surrounded by video screens. On the

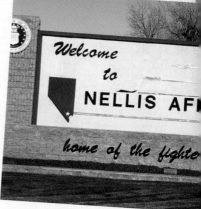

Pilots from Nellis Air Force Base can control Predator planes from thousands of miles away.

At Nellis Air Force base, the pilots keep their eyes on video screens and control the Predators with joysticks. Their instructions are immediately transmitted to Predators thousands of miles away.

screens were images sent via **satellite** from cameras mounted on the Predators.

The pilots kept their eyes glued to the video screens, watching everything on the ground below their Predators. They controlled their planes with joysticks. Their commands were relayed back to their Predator via satellite.

Captain Fred Atwater commanded a group of soldiers in Iraq that controlled about 20 Predators. His soldiers' job was to launch and land these UAVs.

One of his key missions was to escort groups of soldiers on foot patrol. "You weave them through hostile terrain, and get them home safely," Captain Atwater says.

The Predator also played an important role in catching Saddam Hussein, the **dictator** of Iraq. It was used to kill Al Qaeda terrorists in Afghanistan and Pakistan. And it helped find a lost team of Navy SEALs. (SEALs perform secret missions for the Navy.)

But the plane isn't perfect. Like other small planes, it can't fly well in bad weather.

Icy wings have caused many Predator crashes. Newer Predators have de-icing systems. But the plane still crashes at an alarming rate.

A report by the U.S. Congress said the Predator's accident rate is 100 times greater than manned aircraft. The report covered 135 Predator planes used in military operations. Of them, 50 have been lost. And 34 more have had serious accidents. That's a huge rate—particularly when each plane costs $3 million!

UAVS WITH WEAPONS

People have been trying to figure out how to get weapons on board a UAV for a long time.

The idea for sky battles without soldiers isn't new. Here's a look at some of the very early UAVs.

Civil War (1861–1865): An inventor named Charles Perley designed a hot-air balloon that carried a basket of explosives. The basket was hooked to a timer. The timer would cut the balloon's basket. The explosives would drop, hopefully in enemy territory.

Both the North and the South tried to use versions of Perley's balloons. But the design was not effective.

World War I (1914–1918): The U.S. tested a radio-controlled plane that could carry a 300-pound (136-kg) bomb.

World War II (1939–1945): Germany sent guided missiles called V-1s to Great Britain. The U.S. responded by sending out unmanned planes that targeted German launch sites.

The Next Generation

The new wave of UAVs is smaller and faster. But each wave brings new questions.

The next generation of UAVs is led by a plane called the Global Hawk. Cruising at 65,000 feet (19,812 m), the Hawk is harder to gun down than the Predator. But what makes the Hawk truly special is that it can fly itself.

The Predator is a drone. It is controlled entirely by a ground pilot with a joystick. But the Global Hawk can be programmed to fly without help from the ground. Pilots program a flight plan into the Hawk. The plane follows those orders. Still, at $40 million, the Hawk is even more costly than the Predator—and even more likely to crash.

Scientists are also working on mini-planes that can be launched and controlled from short distances. The Marines have tested a five-pound (2.3-kg) UAV called the Dragon Eye. It can be carried in a backpack. It's programmed with a wireless **modem**. It's launched by hand or with a bungee cord. However, it can only stay in the air for an hour.

These U.S. Marines are preparing to hand-launch a Dragon Eye. This UAV is being used for aerial reconnaissance outside the Iraqi city of Fallujah in November 2004.

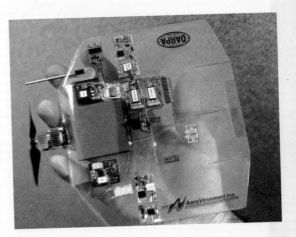

The Black Widow is just the size of a CD. It has a tiny penny-sized camera that takes videos.

The military is also experimenting with a tiny plane called the Black Widow. It works like a Dragon Eye. But it's even smaller—the size of a portable CD player. The six-inch (15.2-cm) flying disk can fly to 600 feet (182.9 m). It takes high-quality videos from a camera the size of a penny. But, like the Dragon Eye, its flight time is limited. Also, bad weather can knock it off course.

There are other plans on the drawing board. The military is working on combat UAVs that can withstand **g-forces** powerful enough to rip a human pilot apart. They're making UAVs that can go where humans would never dare—like into a storm of **chemical weapons** or **nuclear weapons**.

But UAVs have as many critics as fans. Some experts point to their high cost and crash rates. Some consider them science-fiction dreams—not the fighting force of tomorrow.

But the military is moving ahead quickly.

In 2004, the U.S. spent more than $1 billion on UAVs. And experts say the cost will reach $3.35 billion in 2012. Congress has threatened to cut spending on the unmanned planes. But experts believe it's a good bet that UAVs will patrol the skies for years to come. 24/7

EARLY BIRDS

In the 1400s, artist and inventor Leonardo da Vinci planned some UAVs.

Think UAVs are the coolest new high-tech gadgets? So did Leonardo da Vinci—when he came up with the idea 500 years ago! The famed artist and inventor is thought to be the father of unmanned flight. He thought of it in 1488.

Historians have found Leonardo sketches of early UAVs. They think he was inspired to create them by watching birds. He called these designs *Non il volo umano*, which means "Non-human flight." He even designed the first ornithopters, planes that flap their wings and fly like birds.

None of Leonardo's designs ever actually flew—in part because the available materials were too heavy. But later inventors based their UAVs on his ideas.

The Predator got its start in the military. Find out how UAVs are also being used on the home front.

Los Angeles
2006

Sky High

UAVs can soar in domestic skies, too. They can fight forest fires, find lost kids, and even catch crooks.

27

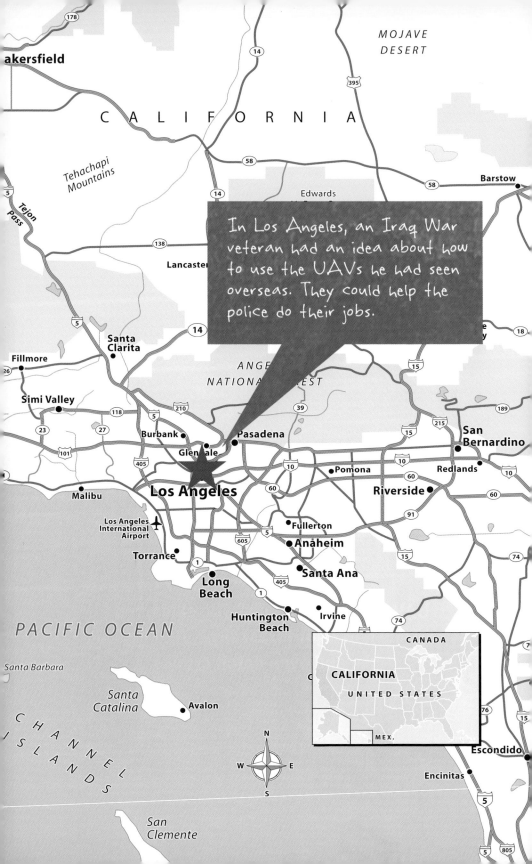

In Los Angeles, an Iraq War veteran had an idea about how to use the UAVs he had seen overseas. They could help the police do their jobs.

A Warplane Goes Home

Could the SkySeer UAV help the Los Angeles Police Department?

They call it the SkySeer. It's a small UAV. It only weighs about three pounds (1.4 kg). And its wingspan is six and a half feet (1.9 m). It flies at just 23 miles (37 km) per hour.

It's small. Also, it's pretty slow. But this tiny, near silent UAV may be the future of unmanned flights.

You see, the SkySeer doesn't fly over war zones.

Instead, it may soar over your head.

This UAV is owned by the Los Angeles Police Department (LAPD). The LAPD wants to use it as a high-tech crime-fighting tool. They see SkySeer UAVs as the future of law enforcement. A UAV could search for fleeing criminals or lost children—in the same way military UAVs hunt for terrorists.

"Here's the coolest thing about SkySeer," explains LAPD's Commander Sid Heal. "It's the first one of its kind built from the ground up for law enforcement. Most of the military ones are bigger and heavier. Ours can fly very low. And it can fly without a pilot."

Sam de la Torre is the inventor of the SkySeer UAV. Here, he's preparing the drone for launch during a June 2006 demonstration flight in Redlands, California.

From Iraq to LA

The same technology used in the Iraqi desert helps build UAVs for LA.

Commander Heal from the LAPD saw UAVs in action while serving with the military in Iraq. He was fascinated by MAVs like the Dragon Eye, planes that were small enough to fit in a soldier's backpack. The swift planes were amazingly quiet. They could fly low and watch people through video cameras.

Heal thought about the huge, loud helicopters he used for police work. He knew that, in some cases, a UAV could do a better job. A police officer could store a UAV in the trunk of his car. It would be ready for action at a moment's notice—maybe even in time to track a fleeing **suspect**.

While Commander Heal was serving in Iraq, he saw a Dragon Eye like this one. That's when he got the idea that the LAPD could use UAVs, too.

When Heal got home, he proposed adding UAVs to the LAPD. He approached a manufacturer to build a SkySeer, based on the same technology he saw in Iraq.

SkySeer folds up like a tent and fits into the trunk of a police car. It's only about six feet (1.8 m) wide. It weighs just three pounds (1.4 kg). The camera in its nose can see about 200 feet (60.1 m) in all directions. It can instantly send pictures to a laptop. It can even make out images in the dark.

With SkySeer, the police can react in an instant when a call comes in for a missing child or a criminal on the run. They don't have to wait for a helicopter.

The Dragon Eye can be controlled from a laptop, as shown here. Heal wanted the SkySeer to use this portable technology as well.

Instead, an officer can jump out of his car, open the trunk, and launch and control SkySeer from a laptop. "You just push the takeoff button, the motor starts up, and you throw it," says SkySeer's inventor Sam de la Torre.

Inventor Sam de la Torre with his SkySeer UAV. This was the first UAV created for use in law enforcement.

Beyond SkySeer

UAVs can patrol borders, protect crops, and help fight forest fires.

SkySeer isn't the only UAV at work in U.S. skies. The National Aeronautics and Space Administration (NASA) has one, too. NASA's sun-powered PathFinder-Plus UAV flew over coffee fields in Hawaii. Its job was to find weeds, dry places, and ripe coffee beans. Because it flew so low, PathFinder could do what other planes couldn't: It could fly below the clouds. That means that PathFinder was able to provide pictures with no clouds in the way.

Another NASA UAV called Altair collects information about whales, air quality, and ocean currents. Altair has also used its cameras and computers to map coastlines. And the U.S. Forest Service envisions using remote-operated planes to beam images of forest fires back to base camps.

The PathFinder-Plus is operated by remote-control. It's also solar-powered. And it can fly much lower than other planes.

Perhaps the biggest nonmilitary use of drones has been as border patrols. The U.S. Customs and Border Protection agency has used a version of the Predator UAV to monitor the U.S./Mexico border. In its first six months, the Predator aided in the arrest of nearly 2,000 illegal immigrants and the seizure of four tons of marijuana, border officials say.

SkySeer in flight over Redlands, California, in 2006 (*left*). This camera (*above*) is placed on the belly of the plane. It takes videos of the ground below.

Grounding UAVs

Critics have issues about UAV safety.

Still, even though UAVs are becoming more common, their nonmilitary use has far to go.

Some experts worry that UAVs pose safety hazards to manned flights. The National Transportation Safety Board fears that the sky just isn't big enough for human pilots to share with UAVs. They want to make sure that UAVs don't stray too close to commercial or private planes—and crash into them.

Others note that a sky filled with unmanned planes carrying video cameras could create privacy issues. Planes that are too small to see and too quiet to hear could take pictures anywhere they wanted. That scares some people who say that the police and the government could use UAVs to spy on anyone.

Meanwhile, the SkySeer has come back down to earth. During a test run in 2006, the LAPD's star plane crashed. The SkySeer was grounded for more tests. 24/7

Making small planes is hard enough. The engineers in the next case are trying to create vehicles that actually fly the way birds do.

Provo, Utah
May 19–20, 2006

Robo-Flies

**Get out your magnifying glass.
These tiny spies are the
biggest thing in UAVs.**

The Battle of the Micro UAVs

Who can create the most effective spy plane ever?

A.J. Kochevar (*right*) launches a tiny MAV during the eighth International Micro Air Vehicle Competition. Behind him is pilot Bret Becker.

At first glance, the Micro Air Vehicle Competition looks like a lot like a model airplane race.

In a hall at Brigham Young University in Provo, Utah, dozens of science scholars from around the country toss planes the size of hummingbirds into the air. Some planes flap their wings and glide through obstacle courses. Others nose-dive straight into the ground.

It looks like good-natured fun. You'd never guess that these bird-sized planes could be the next great invention in modern **espionage**.

Imagine a plane that's so quiet it can't be heard. It's so small it can hardly be seen. It can perch on a branch or a rooftop just like a bird. Or it can travel through a cave by remote control. And the plane has a video camera attached to its nose. It can see and hear everything around it. It's the perfect spy.

That's exactly what the students at the Utah competition were trying to create: the most effective spy plane in history.

Two of those students were Bill Silin and

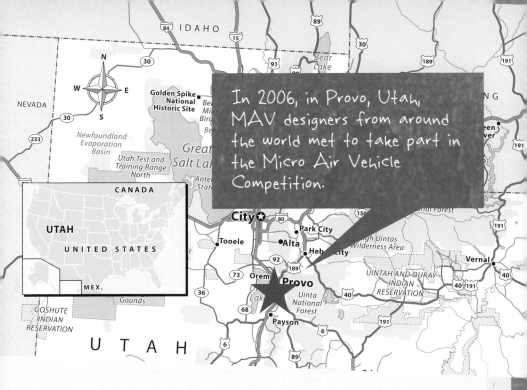

In 2006, in Provo, Utah, MAV designers from around the world met to take part in the Micro Air Vehicle Competition.

U T A H

Bret Becker of the University of Arizona. They worked for years to make ornithopters —planes that imitate the flapping motion of birds. They built the smallest ornithopter in the world. It's just six inches (15.2 cm) long and has a video camera in its nose. It looks like a clever model plane. But it's far from a toy. "Without a doubt," Becker says, "we're building spy planes."

There's only one problem with these super micro spies. No ornithopter has ever really worked before. And even the world's best scientists aren't sure why.

Bill Silin, an aerospace engineering student, prepares to launch an ornithopter. See the blurred wings? They're flapping.

37

Flapping Flight

A plane that flies like a bird could soar in the spy world.

Just why do experts think ornithopters would be the greatest spy invention since the magnifying glass? It's mostly because small spy planes could fly in the same way as birds and insects. And that would be great for spies.

Why? Ordinary planes simply can't do what an ornithopter could. Say a plane could flap its wings like a bird. Then it could perch, hover, or crawl in tight spaces. Bigger and bulkier UAVs fly too fast to go down corridors and make turns.

A tiny, flapping plane—or a micro ornithopter—could explore the hardest-to-reach enemy hideouts. It would also be difficult to detect. A micro ornithopter could perch in a tree and watch and wait for days.

This full-sized ornithopter, the Canadian Flapper, made a test flight in Toronto, Ontario, in July 2006.

It could **eavesdrop** on conversations without ever being seen.

Military officials say the tiny spies would give them an amazing advantage. They'd love to have a UAV that can glide deep within a building to find **hostages** and catch criminals. Right now, the best technology available is robots. And they're large and clumsy.

Still, ornithopters have a long way to go before they rescue anybody. Right now, they're fragile.

Also, scientists still aren't sure how to power a tiny flyer. The smallest micro vehicles rely on batteries. A very tiny UAV can't carry the weight of a battery with enough power to fly it. Batteries, motors, and hardware are just too big and heavy.

Even the most advanced full-sized ornithopter in the world can barely lift off the ground. One of these, the Canadian Flapper, managed to fly for just 14 seconds—a world record!

But perhaps the biggest problem is one that engineers have never solved. To invent planes that fly like birds or bees, engineers have to learn how they do it.

The Flapper stayed in the air for just 14 seconds before wind caused it to crash back onto the runway.

The Great Winged Mystery

It looks so easy. But how do birds and insects actually manage to fly?

To fly, birds and insects flap their wings. This does two things. First, it gives them the lift they need to get off the ground. But it also moves them forward. And, believe it or not, scientists don't totally understand how they can do both at once.

Scientists know how birds and insects get off the ground. Birds use speed and airflow around their wings to create enough lift to fly. Insects are different. To a bee, the air is thick, like water. Experts say insects don't fly as much as "swim" in the air.

But once they are aloft, neither birds nor bees should be able to move forward. How they move has confused scientists for centuries.

Today, researchers think they are close to solving the puzzle. They now know that insects use their wings to create powerful air currents. They "ride" those currents, using them to push their bodies forward. Their wings force air behind them. And the birds and bugs actually get energy from a portion of that wind current. That energy powers their wings. Each flap gives them more strength to go forward.

All the Buzz

Whether they imitate birds or bees, mini UAVs are taking flight.

Even as scientists compete to perfect the smallest ornithopters on earth, others think insects have more buzz than birds. Some experts are working on **entomopters**. Those are planes that fly like insects.

Bugs flap their wings much faster than birds. They can lift quickly off the ground and hover in the air more effectively. At the Georgia Tech Research Institute, one expert has created a micro entomopter that refuels using chemicals from the air.

At the University of California, scientist Michael Dickinson has made what he calls "Robofly." The robotic mini plane flaps with the help of three tiny motors on each tiny wing.

NASA is even testing micro planes that can sprout wings on command.

Back at the Micro Air Vehicle Competition in Utah, Bill Silin and Bret Becker from the University of Arizona were counting on their six-inch (15.2-cm) ornithopter to bring home first prize.

This robofly was designed to imitate the way a fly actually flies. It was developed by researchers at the University of California, Berkeley.

Becker launched the tiny plane by tossing it into the air. Its little wings began to beat. They flapped faster and faster. Soon, he could see nothing but a blur.

Using a joystick, he piloted the plane around two cones. He sped around the course once. Twice. Three times. Seven times. Then, with the battery nearly out of power, Becker steered the plane in a single loop around the cones.

"It's a friendly competition," Silin explains. "But I really want to win. I'm having fun. And I'm also proving that I'm doing my research in the right way. If I do it right, I win."

In the end, Silin got his wish. Their ornithopter won the contest. It was the smallest, lightest, and most controllable flapping plane in the world.

Still, Silin and Becker are trying to make their ornithopter even smaller. Silin thinks it can be about the size of a hummingbird. "In about five years," he says, "we should have a hummingbird plane that can hover and perch." **24/7**

Silin and Becker's ornithopter is six inches (15.2 cm). The central part of the plane (the fuselage) is extremely light. It's made of tiny carbon-fiber rods.

SPY DOWNLOAD

Before you can earn a degree in UAVs, check out more amazing facts about these flying spies.

IN THIS SECTION:

▶ UAVs fly—without pilots—through history;

▶ UAVs and MAVs make the news;

▶ and could a career in UAVs be in your future?

Key Dates in UAVs

UAVs may be cutting-edge. But they aren't brand-new. Take a look at how UAVs have flown through history.

1883 Go Fly a Kite
Douglas Archibald takes the first successful aerial photograph from a kite. Kites will be used in the Spanish-American War of 1898 to snap photos behind enemy lines.

1889 Under (Remote) Control
Nikolai Tesla (*right*) invents radio remote control. He uses it to control a small boat. The same technology will someday fly planes!

1917 Aerial Torpedo
Two Americans invent a stabilizer that keeps aircraft flying straight. That technology paves the way for the first radio-controlled UAV (*left*). Called the Sperry Aerial Torpedo, it can fly 50 miles (80 km) and carry a 300-pound (136-kg) bomb. It's never used in combat.

1939 **UAV Targets**

Hollywood actor and aviation fan Reginald Denny (*right*) develops a large, remote-controlled airplane. Denny's drones take off by slingshot and land with a parachute. The U.S. Air Force orders thousands of them to be used as targets for training anti-aircraft gunners.

1942 **Flapping Flight**

In Germany, a man named Adalbert Schmid builds the first successful manned ornithopter. It uses an engine to flap its wings.

1964 **What a Drone**

The Firebee takes flight. It's one of the first successful drones. The UAV flies on autopilot with radio control. The U.S. Air Force uses the Firebee in the Vietnam War (1959–1975) for everything from dropping propaganda to detecting enemy missiles.

1973 **Arming the Firebee**

Israel perfects the modern UAV by sending a Firebee (*right*) to war. A modified version of the unmanned jet is fit with missiles. During the Yom Kippur War, it leads attacks against Egypt.

1995 **The Predator Strikes**

The star UAV of the U.S. flies its first missions in the Balkans. Now a staple of the Air Force, the Predator has flown in Afghanistan and Iraq. Designed as a spy plane, it now carries missiles and can attack targets.

In the News

Read all about it! UAVs are front-page news.

UAVs Aid in Disaster Relief

PEARLINGTON, MISSISSIPPI—September 14, 2005

After Hurricane Katrina, disaster relief agencies used two unmanned aerial vehicles (UAVs) to search storm-damaged communities in Mississippi. They were looking for trapped survivors.

It was one of the first uses of UAVs for disaster search and rescue.

The storm pushed houses into the middle of the street and blocked rescuers from reaching Pearlington. But the UAVs gave rescuers a broad overview of the disaster area. It showed them where help was needed.

A Drone Helicopter

One of the UAVs is a four-foot (1.2-m) airplane that's launched by hand and is equipped with cameras. The other UAV was a camera-equipped, miniature, electric helicopter called a T-Rex. The helicopter can hover at nearly 250 feet (76.2 m). It can zoom its camera to peek inside windows or scan rooftops.

Within two hours, the vehicles provided rescuers with information showing that no survivors had been trapped.

After Hurricane Katrina devastated the Mississippi coast, UAVs were able to take videos that helped with search and rescue.

A Global Hawk begins its descent. This pilotless plane may help the U.S. government protect airports from missile attacks.

Drones Could Defend Airports

WASHINGTON, D.C.—March 22, 2007

The air traffic over airports might get a little crowded. And that's good news.

The Department of Homeland Security and the military will test whether UAVs can protect the nation's busiest airports from terrorist attacks. They plan to test-fly drones 65,000 feet (19,812 m) above the airports.

According to the plan, the drones would guard planes from being shot down by terrorists with shoulder-fired missiles.

Missile-Warning Systems

The drones would be fitted with missile-warning systems. They'd also have anti-missile lasers that could send missiles off course, Homeland Security officials said.

A rocket launcher fires an almost invisible ultraviolet light at its target. The UAV could detect the light and fire an anti-missile laser. The laser would lock on to the missile and knock it out.

The military has been testing anti-missile laser systems for the last four years. They've attached the systems to the bellies of Federal Express cargo planes to see how well they hold up.

The plan is code-named "Project Chloe" after a character on Homeland Security Secretary Michael Chertoff's favorite TV show, 24.

Eyes in the Sky

UAVs have gone to war and helped in disasters. But they may be most valuable as photographers. Here's a collection of photos taken by UAVs.

A Watch Dog in Iraq

These photos were taken by a Predator drone in Iraq. They uncovered weapons hideouts for Iraqi militants. In this picture, Iraqi tanks on trucks are being hidden near homes and mosques.

The Predator over the Balkans

In the early 1990s, there was terrible violence in an area in Eastern Europe called the Balkans. NATO, a group of 26 countries, sent Predators there to do reconnaissance. The top photo to the left was taken in 1993 and shows an ammunition plant. The photo below it, taken in 1995, shows the plant after NATO bombed it.

UAVs to the Rescue!

In late October 2006, the Altair UAV was dispatched to southern California to monitor the deadly Esperanza fire. The fire killed five firefighters and destroyed 34 houses. It raged over 61 miles (98.2 km). NASA sent a UAV to take these photos of the blaze. That helped firefighters track and control it.

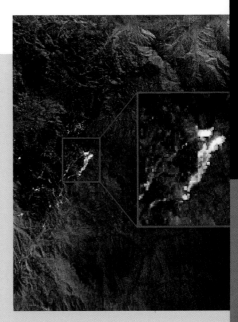

Katrina Relief

Hurricane Katrina ripped through the Gulf Coast in 2006. Rescue workers used unmanned drones to fly through storm-wrecked sites, searching for survivors. In many cases, the UAVs went into areas that rescue workers couldn't reach. In this image, a UAV snapped photos of the storm's devastation in Pearlington, Mississippi.

Up Close and Personal with the Predator

UAV designers try everything to make their planes light, strong, and easy to steer.

OUTSIDE THE PREDATOR

length: 27 feet (8.3 m)
height: 6.9 feet (2.1 m)
wingspan: 48.7 feet (14.8 m)

engine

The 101-horsepower engine on the back of the Predator is the same engine used on many snowmobiles.

SAR Unit

The SAR—synthetic aperture radar—helps the plane fly in any weather.

propeller

The propeller in the rear lifts the plane and helps drive it forward.

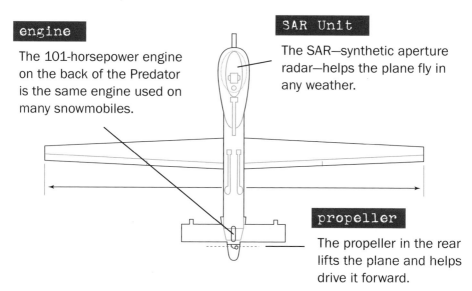

INSIDE THE PREDATOR

Satellite Communications Antenna

This antenna lets the pilot-less plane receive commands from the ground station through a satellite.

Battery Packs

Two 8-pound (3.6-kg), 14-amp-hour battery packs act as backup power supplies in case the engine fails.

Engine Cooling Fan

Conventional antifreeze—just like the material used in most cars—cools the engine.

Fuel Tanks

The Predator's two fuel tanks carry up to 600 pounds (272.2 kg) of aircraft engine fuel.

Global Positioning Systems

The Predator has two Global Positioning System (GPS) antennas that help the plane locate its prey.

HELP WANTED:
Micro Aerial Vehicle Designer

Interested in designing MAVs? Here's more information about the field.

Bill Silin is a PhD candidate in aerospace engineering at the University of Arizona.

Q&A: BILL SILIN

24/7: Describe what you do.

BILL SILIN: I design and build miniature ornithopters—flying machines that flap like birds.

24/7: How did you get started building ornithopters?

SILIN: It started as a hobby. Back in 1987, I started working on small flying models.

24/7: What's so great about building tiny flapping model planes?

SILIN: People have been trying to create flying machines for thousands of years. But no one could do it. It's a challenging problem. And it's even more challenging when you deal with very small parts.

24/7: Tell us about the MAV competitions.

SILIN: The goal of the competition is not just to fly the machine. It must be small, fast, and easy to control. Our ornithopters are very easy to control. You pilot it with a joystick. And we installed a camera in it, so you can see where you're going.

24/7: What does it take to get into a career like yours, building MAVs?

SILIN: The most important thing is that you have to be ready to learn a lot. The nice thing about this field is you're the pilot, designer, and builder. But that means you need to understand something about aerodynamics, technologies, design, electronics, plastics. Usually, previous experience with building flying models helps. But I think the most important thing is the desire and the interest and the ability to learn.

24/7: Do you need a college degree to build a MAV?

SILIN: You don't need a degree to do this, but it helps. When you study aerospace, you see direct connections between the lessons and the flying machines.

Do you have what it takes to be work with UAVS? Take this totally unscientific quiz to find out!

1 **How do you feel about making model airplanes?**
a) My shelves are covered with them!
b) They were fun for a while. But then I got bored and found a new hobby.
c) Hmm. Insert flap A into slot B? Yikes! I'm gonna watch TV.

2 **Do you know what an engineer does?**
a) Chemical, electrical, industrial, or mechanical? Or maybe you mean aerospace engineers?
b) It's someone who uses science to solve problems, right?
c) You mean the guy who drives a train?

3 **Do you know what drag, lift, weight, and thrust are?**
a) Those are the four forces that govern flight. Try a hard question.
b) It sounds like they have something to do with airplanes.
c) Sure I know them. I have all their CDs.

4 **UAV designers often test the same plane over and over. How patient are you?**
a) I'll keep trying till it works.
b) I'll try anything once. Even twice. But I have my limits.
c) I don't even want to watch reruns!

5 **Are you interested in state-of-the-art technology?**
a) I'm a total techno-geek! I love to learn by reading, studying—and doing.
b) I'll learn it for my science test. And I'll forget it the next day.
c) Does it have something to do with video games?

YOUR SCORE

Give yourself 3 points for every "a" you chose. Give yourself 2 points for every "b" you chose. Give yourself 1 point for every "c" you chose.

If you got **13–15 points**, you might have UAV design in your future.

If you got **10–12** points, don't rule out a career in the micro spy world.

If you got **5–9** points, look for another job!

1 2 3 4 5 6 7 8 9 10

HOW TO GET STARTED...NOW!

It's never too early to start working toward your goals.

GET AN EDUCATION

► Focus on science classes, particularly physics. Math skills—algebra and calculus—will also come in handy.
► Start looking at colleges. Target schools with good engineering programs.
► Keep up with UAVs in the news. Unmanned planes are always making headlines. Learn what you can from newspapers, CNN, and Internet sites.
► Read anything you can about UAVs. See the books and Web sites in the Resources section on pages 56–58.
► Graduate from high school!

NETWORK!

► Look into UAV networks in your area. Join model airplane clubs. You can meet other aerial enthusiasts!
► Write to UAV associations and manufacturers. They can send you info on how to break into the field.

GET AN INTERNSHIP

► Look for an internship with aeronautic agencies.
► Join associations that encourage young people like the National Aeronautic Association's Air Youth of America, the University Aviation Association, or the Academy of Model Aeronautics at Purdue University.

LEARN ABOUT OTHER JOBS IN AERONAUTICS

From designers to engineers to pilots, there are many jobs in the UAV world.

Resources

Looking for more information? Here are some resources you don't want to miss!

PROFESSIONAL ORGANIZATIONS

Central Intelligence Agency (CIA)
www.cia.gov
Office of Public Affairs
Washington, DC 20505
PHONE: 703-482-0623
FAX: 703-482-1739

The CIA was created in 1947 when President Harry Truman signed the National Security Act. The organization works to collect information that will help keep the United States safe. It also engages in research and development of high-level technology for gathering intelligence around the world.

Federal Bureau of Investigation (FBI)
www.fbi.gov
J. Edgar Hoover Building
935 Pennsylvania Avenue, NW
Washington, DC 20535
PHONE: 202-324-3000

The FBI works to protect and defend the United States from terrorism and foreign threats. It also upholds the criminal laws of the United States and provides leadership for federal, state, and local law enforcement.

National Aeronautics and Space Administration (NASA)
www.nasa.gov
Suite 5K39
Washington, DC 20546-0001
PHONE: 202-358-0001
E-MAIL: public-inquiries@hq.nasa.gov

The mission of this organization is to pioneer the future in space exploration, scientific discovery, and aeronautics research.

U.S. Department of Homeland Security (DHS)
www.dhs.gov
Washington, DC 20528
PHONE: 202-282-8000

This department was created in 2002 to protect the United States from terrorist attacks.

U.S. Department of State
www.state.gov
2201 C Street, NW
Washington, DC 20520
PHONE: 202-647-4000

The mission of the U.S. State Department is to create a more secure, democratic, and prosperous world for people in the United States and the international community. The people at the State Department use diplomacy, negotiation, and intelligence to work with other countries throughout the world.

WEB SITES

AV Aerovironment
www.avsuav.com

Aerovironment is the company that built Black Widow. It's one of the top MAV companies.

The Defense Review
www.defensereview.com

This is an online magazine loaded with information about defense technology.

Global Security/ Intelligence/MAVS
www.globalsecurity.org/intell/ systems/mav.htm

Global Security is not a military site. But it includes information about all kinds of military technology including MAVs.

MLB Company
www.spyplanes.com

This is a major manufacturer of spy planes; the Web site has a video demo.

NASA/Unmanned Area Vehicles
uav.wff.nasa.gov

This is NASA's page overview of UAVs.

NOVA: Spies Fly
www.pbs.org/wgbh/nova/spiesfly

This Web site has terrific photos and information about the history of UAVs and war.

Student Unmanned Aerial Competition
uav.navair.navy.mil/seafarers/default.htm

This is a Web site for the 2007 SUAC, an amateur competition involving UAV design and demonstrations.

Technology Trends
www.primidi.com/2005/04/01.html

This site focuses on MAV technology and its applications.

Today's Military/UV Operations Specialists
www.todaysmilitary.com
(click on "Engineering Careers" in search bar, then click on "Unmanned Vehicle (UV) Operations Specialist")

This is the Web site for the U.S. military. It includes information about all kinds of engineering and technical jobs, including jobs related to MAVs.

UAV Flight Systems
www.uavflight.com

This company is a developer of UAV technology.

U.S. Navy/UAV Demonstration
http://uav.navair.navy.mil

See a UAV demo on the Navy Web site.

BOOKS

Fridell, Ron. *Spy Technology*. Minneapolis: Lerner Publications, 2006.

Graham, Ian, and N. J. Hewetson. *Planes, Rockets, and Other Flying Machines* (Fast Forward). Danbury, Conn.: Franklin Watts, 2000.

January, Brendan. *CIA: U.S. Government and Military*. Danbury, Conn.: Franklin Watts, 2003.

Owen, David. *Spies: The Undercover World of Secrets, Gadgets and Lies*. Richmond Hill, Ont.: Firefly Books, 2004.

Schleifer, Jay. *Spy Planes* (Wings). Mankato, Minn.: Capstone Press, 1996.

Sweetman, Bill. *High-Altitude Spy Planes: The U-2s* (War Planes). Mankato, Minn.: Capstone Press, 2001.

A

aeronautics (ayr-oh-NAW-tiks) *noun* the study of flight and aircraft

autonomous (aw-TAH-nuh-muhs) *adjective* independent; describing a plane that can fly itself

B

backpackable (BAK-pak-uh-buhl) *adjective* small and light enough to carry in a backpack

Black Widow (blak WIH-doh) *noun* the smallest UAV; it takes high-quality videos with a penny-sized camera

bungee (BUHN-jee) *noun* a stretchy cord sometimes used to launch MAVs

C

chemical weapons (KEM-ih-kul WEH-punz) *noun* weapons that are made of poisons and dangerous gases

cockpit (KOK-pit) *noun* the place in a plane from which it is controlled

contractors (kon-TRAK-turz) *noun* companies that turn basic UAV designs into military tools

D

dictator (DIK-tay-tur) *noun* a ruler who has complete control over a country; dictators do not have to answer to the people and can treat them any way they want to.

Dragon Eye (DRAH-gun eye) *noun* a type of MAV that flies itself and is hand-launched

drone (drone) *noun* a plane that is controlled by a ground pilot with a joystick

E

eavesdrop (EEVZ-drop) *verb* to listen secretly to something that's said privately

engineer (en-jihn-EER) *noun* a person who uses scientific knowledge to solve problems

entomopters (EN-toh-mop-turz) *noun* airplanes that are designed to fly like insects. The prefix *ento* has to do with insects.

Dictionary

espionage (ESS-pee-uh-nahzh) *noun* the act of using spies to gain information about the plans and activities of other groups, armies, and countries

F

fabricators (fah-brih-KAY-turz) *noun* people who build UAVs

G

g-forces (JEE-fors-ez) *noun* effects of gravity or acceleration on a person or machine

Global Hawk (GLO-bul hawk) *noun* a kind of spy plane that can fly itself

H

hostages (HOS-tij-ez) *noun* people who are captured and held in exchange for certain demands, like money or other people's freedom

I

infrared (IN-frah-rehd) *adjective* describing a camera that can work in the dark

intelligence (in-TEL-uh-jens) *noun* information about an enemy or a possible enemy

J

joystick (JOY-stik) *noun* a lever that operates an airplane (or other device) by forward, backward, and side-to-side motions

M

MAV (EM-aye-vee) *noun* a UAV that is super-small and controlled by radio. It is short for *micro aerial vehicle*.

missiles (MIH-suhlz) *noun* weapons that are shot or projected to strike something at a distance

missions (MIH-shunz) *noun* special jobs or tasks

modem (MOH-dum) *noun* a device that converts signals from one kind of machine to another, like between a phone and a computer

N

nuclear weapons (NOO-klee-ur WEH-punz) *noun* highly destructive weapons that get their power from atomic reactions

O

ornithopter (ORN-ih-thop-tur) *noun* an airplane that mimics the way birds fly. Ornithopters have wings that flap.

P

Predator (PREH-duh-tur) *noun* a kind of UAV that carries two laser-guided missiles for attacks

propeller (pruh-PEH-luhr) *noun* a device that has a central hub and rotating blades; it moves ships, planes, and other machines forward.

R

reconnaissance (ree-KOHN-uh-sins) *noun* the collection of preliminary intelligence, usually by visual inspection or secret observation

remote-controlled (reh-MOTE kun-TROLD) *adjective* describing something that is powered or controlled from a distance and usually with an electronic signal

S

satellite (sah-tuh-LYTE) *noun* an object that orbits the earth and is sometimes used to take pictures or send signals

suspect (SUSS-pekt) *noun* a person whom law enforcement officials think may have committed a crime

T

terrorists (TAIR-ur-ists) *noun* people who commit violent acts and use fear as a way to control other people, usually for political reasons

U

UAV (YOO-aye-vee) *noun* an aircraft with no pilot onboard. It is short for *unmanned aerial vehicle*. A UAV can fly by remote control, or it can follow a preprogrammed flight plan.

Index

24 television show, 47

aeronautics, 9
Afghanistan, 21, 22, 45
air currents, 40
Al Qaeda terrorist group, 20, 22
Altair UAV, 32, 49
Archibald, Douglas, 44
Atwater, Fred, 22

backpackables, 9, 12, 24, 30
Balkans, 45, 48, *48*
batteries, 12, 39, 42, 51, *51*
Becker, Bret, *36*, 37, 41–42
birds, 9, 13, 26, 36, 37, 38, 39,
   40, 41, 52
Black Widow UAV, 12–13, *13*, 16,
   16, 25, *25*
Boeing 720 UAV, 16, *16*
border patrols, *23*, 33
Bosnia, 48, *48*
Brigham Young University, 36
bungee cord, 9, 12, 24

cameras, 9, 11, 13, 19, *20*, 21,
   22, 25, 30, 31, 32, *33*, 34,
   36, 37, 44, 46, *48*, 53
chemical weapons, 25
Chertoff, Michael, 47
Civil War, 23
cockpit, 19
commercial air traffic, 34
communications antennas, 51, *51*
Condor UAV, 16
contractors, 14
cooling fans, 51, *51*
cost, 10, 11, 13, 23, 24, 25, 26
crashes, 10, 11, 12, 22, 23, 24,
   25, 34, *39*

D-21 UAV, 16
de-icing systems, 23
Denny, Reginald, 45, *45*

Department of Homeland Security,
   47
Dickinson, Michael, 41
Dragon Eye MAV, 12, *12*, 24, *24*,
   30, *30*, *31*
drones, 9, 33, 45, 46, 47

eavesdropping, 39
education, 53, 55
Egypt, 45
engineers, 9, 14, *37*, 39, 52–53
engines, 45, 50, *50*, 51, *51*
entomopters, 41
Esperanza fire, 49, *49*

fabricators, 14
Fallujah, Iraq, *24*
Firebee UAV, 45, *45*
fuel tanks, 51, *51*

g-forces, 25
Georgia Tech Research Institute, 41
Global Hawk UAV, 11, *11*, 24, *47*
Global Positioning System (GPS),
   51, *51*

Heal, Sid, 29, 30
height, 10, 11, 50
Helios UAV, 16, *16*
Hellfire missiles, 10, 18–19, *19*, 20
Hurricane Katrina, 46, *46*, 49, *49*
Hussein, Saddam, 22

infrared cameras, 9
insects, 40, 41
intelligence, 8
internships, 55
Iraq, *20*, 21, 22, *24*, 30, *30*, 45,
   48, *48*
Israel, 45

joysticks, 9, 10, 14, 20, 22, 24,
   42, 53

kites, 44
Kochevar, A. J., *36*

length, 10, 11, 12, 50
Leonardo da Vinci, 26
Los Angeles, California, *28*, 29, 31

Before I started this book, I had never heard of UAVs. I was surprised to see that they looked exactly like model airplanes. I was even more surprised to find out that college kids design and build some of the world's fastest UAVs.

When I talked to Bill Silin and Bret Becker, the ornithopter designers at the University of Arizona, I learned a lot about why students think it's fun to design and build their own UAVs. The International MAV Competition sounded very cool. I like the idea of traveling to other countries. And the winners get lots of support from their schools.

They may look like toys, but UAVs are serious business. They're used for everything from warfare to disaster relief. Researching this book really opened my eyes to the many uses of UAV. Some are regrettably necessary, like spying on enemies in battle or even launching an attack on terrorists. Others are remarkable advances, like saving people after Hurricane Katrina. Still others are troubling. Privacy advocates worry that UAVs will make it easier for the government, the police, or even criminals to spy on us.

With so many great uses for these amazing machines, I hope we can make sure that they always fly responsibly.

SPECIAL THANKS TO: Bill Silin and Bret Becker, student micro ornithopter designers with the University of Arizona; Cmdr. Sid Heal, LAPD

CONTENT ADVISER: Steven Aftergood, Director of the Project on Government Secrecy, Federation of American Scientists